A Traveller's Guide to

Gower Ghosts

Written & Illustrated

by Chris Elphick

Copyright © 2021 Chris Elphick

All rights reserved.

ISBN: 9798749872200

Cover art: Rhossili Bay, Gower by Chris Elphick

All writing, art and photography contained in this publication are copyright © Chris Elphick 2021 and must not be reproduced without the written consent of the author

Llanrhidian Church – Home to the Llanelen Cursed Stones

Introduction

It would not be difficult to imagine the spring or summer visitor to Gower finding little evidence of the dark, brooding tapestry of emotions this stretch of South-West Wales countryside can embroider upon the mind. Gower is a place for holiday-making to these sunshine tourists, for bathing on its numerous sandy bays or picnicking upon its vast open common land. Notions of ghosts and things that go bump in the night lurking amongst the peninsula's beaches, churchyards and charming rural villages seem nothing but ridiculous. But with the chilling of its air and the lengthening of its shadows, a richly connotative aura rises from Gower's soil. Riding upon the wind to every nook and corner of the peninsula and beyond into the treacherous sea that bludgeons its coast, this bleak winter atmosphere easily lends itself to persuading those that tread its winter landscape into at least half believing the legends and ghost stories of ancient Gower.

The Gower peninsula's character is dualistic. But though and an entire library of books is devoted to the more carefree aspects of its personality, publications concerning Gower's darker nature are scant in their number. It is to address the apparent imbalance in the coverage of Gower's darker mood that this publication concerns itself. Within the shadows of Gower's sunny charms hides a fascinating history of the supernatural. In recounting the various tales that follow, I

hope that this mysterious realm compels and delights in a manner equal, if not transcendent, to the pleasures of the peninsula's more familiar celebrity.

Chris Elphick, 2021

The Bury Estuary, Low Tide

The Bury Estuary, a vast expanse of flat marshland with crisscrossing channels and wandering ponies, dominates the northern half of the Gower Peninsula. Driving westwards from the village of Penclawdd, the marsh to your right, the countryside becomes increasingly rural and anachronistic. Much of this land is lost to the sea at high tide,

The Bury Estuary, High Tide

and before it became overly silted, this scene was once one of merchant ships and seaside industry. Already, before even leaving Penclawdd, the more sensitive amongst us will feel our imaginations stir from the sterile modernity of urban life.

To our left, rolling hills adorned with patchwork fields give way to a string of intermittent housing, hamlets and villages – Penclawdd, Crofty, Llanmorlais and Llanrhidian. Between these latter two villages once blossomed another rural community, that of Llanelen. Nothing but a few stones mark the site of this old hamlet today, its history made sparse by its abandonment and fascinating by superstition. According to legend, Llanelen was abandoned sometime in the 17th Century after an old shipping vessel carrying the plague shored up in the estuary! Local folklore also states any stone taken from the site of the ancient hamlet's graveyard is cursed!.

Llanrhidian Church

The Cursed Stones of Llanelen

With little left to see on the site of the Llanelen's hamlet itself, let's follow the old marsh lane that skirts the estuary after Crofty and make our first stop on our tour through Gower's old ghost stories in the village of Llanrhidian. We can park outside the medieval church, where a couple of small stone plaques from the lost Llanelen graveyard are cemented into the gate post. These small plaques are rumoured to be cursed and are best left untouched, perhaps understandable considering the devastating history of the village where they once resided.

One of Llanelen's Cursed Stones

Llanelen's Second Graveyard Plaque – Both Stones Can Be Found Embedded in the Gatepost of Llanrhidian Church

Late one night, many years ago, another of Gower's violent storms raged over the peninsula. Struggling against the severe conditions, a cargo ship, its name lost to present-day memory, floundered in the rough Atlantic currents off West Gower. With a great wind threatening the ship with splintering its timbers and scattering its cargo to the hammering waves, the vessel's crew decided to harbour off the Burry Estuary. The storm was an impressive foe, however. And, as they rounded the headland towards the marsh, the ship finally lost its battle against the vehement elements. The ruined ship, its cargo of livestock and fruits and the poor wretched sailors who clung for their dear lives to the floating debris that now scattered the sea were washed slowly inland towards the estuarine village of Llanelen.

Savaged by the freezing water and the severity of the currents, which dragged their struggling bodies beneath the angry waves, only seven of the thirty-two sailors washed ashore that awful night had any vestige of life still beating within their saline drenched chests.

Having escaped the cruel sea, the survivors scrambled from the twisted tideline debris of broken wood and tangled knots of human and cattle bodies and crawled their way from the estuarine shore along a cockleshell lane towards the sleeping village of Llanelen.

Wrapped in the darkness of a late winter's night, the inhabitants of Llanelen woke to the woeful cries of the survivors of the wrecked ship stumbling into their hamlet. The sailors were shown kindly hospitality by the villagers, who took them into their hearts, fed and clothed them and offered them temporary residence in their homes. At the first light of dawn, the villagers gathered the bodies of the drowned sailors and gave them all a Christian burial in the grounds of Llanelen Churchyard.

With the souls of the poor departed sailors rested in the arms of God, a messenger was set forth from the village with the order to ride to the nearest port to give news of the tragic wrecking to other visiting vessels so that word could be sent back to the families of its crew. The seven surviving sailors remained at the village while recovering from what seemed like severe influenza brought on, it appeared, from the ravages of their ordeal.

However, it was not long before this apparent 'flu' virus proved itself to be a particularly virulent condition. And, for their kind-hearted endeavours, each and every inhabitant of Llanelen were rewarded with the same illness.

Just days after the funerals of the sailors drowned at sea, another mass burial announced the awful true identity of the disease. And within a week, the entire population of Llanelen had died - from the plague!

That bewitchment still attaches itself to the grounds where the village once stood is further evidenced by the tale of a farmer who, whilst wandering around the ruined site, found a dressed stone amongst the rubble and took it away with him for use on his farm. Every night thereafter, his sleep was disturbed by the sound of the rock rolling restlessly around the farmyard. And his sleep was not restored until the stone was returned to the site where it rightfully belonged. Again not unexpectedly, there is also a ghost attached to this forlorn area - a spectral lady in white who is said to roam the various debris and trees that has sprung up around here, weeping for the village where she once lived so happily.

The Welcome to Town Inn, Llanrhidian

A small village green separates Llanrhidian Church from the *Welcome to Town Inn*. History weighs heavy upon the senses here and the two impressive megalithic standing stones, which rise from the manicured grass, call for a quiet and solemn reflection of the past.

The *Welcome to Town Inn,* Llanrhidian, was once the meeting place for the *Gower United Association for the Prosecution of Felons'* annual dinner. This group of landowners and farmers were responsible for the rewards offered for the apprehension of local criminals. It disbanded in 1892 after a very quiet last 34 years of service - its last

The Upper Standing Stone, Llanrhidian Village Green

The Lower Standing Stone, Llanrhidian Village Green

active case being that of sheep stealing in 1856. The public house/restaurant is reputed to be haunted, and it is the figure of a coachman whom some believe had associations with this society that haunts this pub today. He has been glimpsed on numerous occasions occupying a table near the front window of this quiet establishment.

The *Welcome to Town Inn*, Llanrhidian

We now follow the lane to the top of the hill from the village green and turn right towards our next spot of supernatural interest, which nestles in the picturesque village of Cheriton.

Glebe House—Cheriton

Glebe House, Cheriton

Glebe House was built in the 14th Century and is the oldest inhabited building on the Gower Peninsula. Over the centuries, the Grade II listed building has been utilised as a centre for the Knights Hospitallers, a Rectory for the adjacent church and as a farmhouse. The building is best viewed from the beautifully atmospheric churchyard it stands next to.

Cheriton Church

The Rector of Cheriton Church (1751-1787), John Williams, is perhaps best remembered for the time he was called in to exorcise the ghost of a previous tenant of Glebe House when she returned from the grave to haunt the property. The somewhat noisy spirit was that of a woman who had once worked the farmland here and had made a name for herself for giving short measure in her sale of dairy produce to the other villagers. The new inhabitants of Glebe House were being terrified by the apparition of this woman, who went around the home crying mournfully, "Weight and measure. Weight and measure," rattling the kitchen china and producing awful sounds of bumping and the rushing of air. In desperation, the family went to the Rev. John Williams, and on hearing of the unnatural disturbances, he agreed to carry out an exorcism on the property.

Shutting himself in the room where the ghost commonly manifested itself, John Williams took a whole two days and nights to grapple with the spirit. Cracking his whip to control her fierce temper and reciting Latin prayers for the entire duration of the marathon exorcism, the Rector finally got the better of the ghost, whom he then ordered to make ropes of sand in the nearby burrows of Broughton Bay.

It is difficult to imagine a more idyllic and serene hamlet than Cheriton. Such a disturbance as the exorcism of Glebe House seems at odds with the tranquil atmosphere so endemic here. Its beauty is such that it feels burdensome to draw oneself away from the place. But we may linger a little longer. Take a quick walk to the edge of the churchyard, on the opposite side to Glebe House. On the other side of the stream, once stood a 17th Century mansion, complete with its own spring. In its time, Cradock Well, now lost to sight, was well known for its supernatural powers. Locals would drop gifts of pins and other votive offerings into its waters to gain favour from whatever spirits lived there.

It is now time to leave Cheriton, but our next stop is only a few minutes' drive from here. We are heading uphill again to visit another medieval church – that of St. Madoc, in the quiet village of Llanmadoc.

Llanmadoc Church

Llanmadoc Church, North Gower

Overlooking a large expanse of the North Gower coastline, the medieval Church in Llanmadoc is usually a scene of rustic tranquility. However, this was not the case on one particularly stormy evening in 1868. The village choir, gathered within the Church walls for their evening practice, were on fine form, their voices raised to combat the sound of thunder and heavy rain that fell from the heavens above them. The Reverend, and local historian, J.D. Davies was present at the time, and he recorded the following disturbance in his book 'The History of West Gower':

"...suddenly an indescribable scream of terror was heard in the churchyard, as of one in the last extremity of mortal fear. I immediately ran out to see what was the matter, and saw a young lad, whom I knew very well, standing in the middle of the

walk, not far from the porch, with his face not only blanched, but actually distorted with fright."

Ushered into the Church, the young man proved inconsolable for a long time afterwards and sat upon a pew a gibbering wreck as he told the Reverend and the gathered choir of the ghost he had seen shuffling around the gravestones outside.

With no earlier record of any haunting at Llanmadoc Church, the Reverend and the choir could make no sense of the terrified lad's account of the ghostly figure of a drenched man. And it was with a sense of bewildered disbelief in the young man's bizarre encounter that the Church finally emptied that evening, and the Reverend and his villagers braved the storm to head back to their various homesteads for the night.

Unbeknown at the time of this bizarre incident, the storm had turned the sea at the bottom of the village into a violent rage, wrecking sixteen ships upon the bay at Whiteford Sands. Countless lives were lost that fateful evening, and the bodies of all the drowned sailors were only discovered along the tideline of the beach the following morning. One can only imagine the thoughts of the Reverend, the village choir and the poor witness of the ghostly apparition (which matched the appearance of the drenched dead men on the beach) when they learned of the disaster.

Sunset at Llanmadoc Church

It is now time to head downhill from Llanmadoc Church to the honesty-box field car park for the next part of our journey around Gower's old ghost stories.

Whiteford Sands

It is a fair walk down to our next destination, to explore the large expanse of sand, dune and pinewood plantations of Whiteford Sands.

The Skeletal Remains of Whiteford Lighthouse

This is a disquietingly lonely bay located on the northwest extremity of North Gower. The long, sandy beach is backed by immense dunes and pine woodland and separates the rough Atlantic Ocean from the Burry Estuary. Given its somewhat isolated location, it is little wonder that the place has gained something of a reputation for being haunted.

The beach at Whiteford, located beneath the distant village of Llanmadoc, has seen more than its fair share of tragedies – the bay was strewn with the drownd bodies of seamen after an almighty storm in January 1868 wrecked 16 coal ships on the coast here. Surprisingly, the haunting Whiteford Sands is most renowned for has nothing to do with this or any other of the numerous maritime misadventures for which the area is noted.

Whiteford Sands is Notorious for the Unexploded Bombs that Regularly Wash Up Along its Shoreline

For a location with such an open vista, affording views over the entire northern coastline of the Gower Peninsula, it is, perhaps, strange how the ghostly happenings of Whiteford Sands seems to be an audio-only phenomenon. It is as though some dark occurrence long ago was recorded on the wind and is replayed when conditions are auspicious.

Unexploded WW2 Artillery Shell, Whiteford Sands

A unique feature to this haunting, alone amongst all the hauntings recorded in *Gower Ghosts*, is that the author of this ghostly guide has encountered the unsetting phenomenon.

Late one evening, many years ago now, my wife and I were camping amongst the burrows near the old Whiteford lighthouse. The mood was already one of apprehension as, along this stretch of beach, uncomfortably close to our night's camp, were many artillery shells deposited here by an earlier tide. These bombs are regularly washed up along Whiteford Sands and remind the visitor of the days when the region was used as target practice by the R.A.F. during World War 2. Along with the uncertainty of whether these shells were live or not or whether the camp had been pitched high enough to escape the full height of the next incoming tide, the brooding iron skeleton of Whiteford Lighthouse struck a particularly unsettling figure during the evening and early dusk. Under its unnerving watchful gaze, an early night was unanimously decided upon.

Settling inside our tent, I fastened the doorway tight against the increasing chill of the late summer's night breeze. However, as I lowered the tent zip, there suddenly rose the sound of galloping hooves heading in our direction! The sound of the hooves grew until the fear of being trampled in the tent became a terrifying possibility.

With the clattering hooves now deafening and right upon our camp, we made ourselves ready for a rapid escape. Scrambling from the tent, the heavy pounding of hooves upon compact sand came to an abrupt and unusual halt, the sound cutting out from a thunderous roar, as though the stampeding creature was only centimetres from trampling us to complete and utter as well as eerie complete silence within a fraction of a second.

Whitford Lighthouse, North Gower

Shocked and in disbelief at the situation we found ourselves in, we both scanned the land around us, readying ourselves to dive away from the animal's stampede. The altitude at which we set our camp on Whiteford Burrows allowed for a clear and complete 360-degree study of the countryside that surrounded us. Although it was now dusk, the summer's night sky glowed a heavy but clear shade of blue, and the complete length of Whiteford Sands was also easily discernible – as was the dune system of Whiteford Burrows. But nothing across the entire terrain around us explained the sound of galloping hooves that had generated so much genuine alarm in us.

A Moonlit Whiteford Sands

Perplexed and uneasy, we reluctantly returned to our tent, our hearts thundering in our chests almost as loud as the phantom galloping that had so disturbed us.

Whilst no legend or ghost story related to Whiteford Sands was known by the author at this time, later research into the area revealed the curious event was a well-known phenomenon here. Over the years, many, it seemed, have heard the galloping of ghostly hooves along Whiteford Sands, the sound always beginning from the direction of Broughton Bay, some 3km distant, growing to deafening proportions before suddenly disappearing into the ether again. Reading the various accounts and ghostly explanations for the phenomena filled my heart with an indescribable chill as my supernatural encounter with some rampaging animal was remembered in detail once more.

There are numerous tales concerning the origins of this strange ghostly sound. Some range from thousands of years ago when Mammoths roamed the land here. The fact that the sounds have been connected with a ghostly mammoth gives a fine example of just how loud the sound of the galloping can be:

Returning with the day's shellfish collection off Whiteford Sands, the cockle women drove their donkeys and carts home along the Burry Estuary. Suddenly, there arose the clamour of galloping hooves. Looking back to whence this cacophony arose, the cockle women and their donkeys alike were terrified at the appearance of a huge woolly mammoth, intent on running them all down. The cockle women could offer little fight against the behemoth animal, whose mighty tusks soon tore them all, donkey included, to bloody shreds. The incident closed Whiteford Sands to industry until desperate for more money, a few of the cockle women returned to the large cockle beds. But each time poverty drew the shellfish pickers back to the sands, the distant sound of the giant mammoth's approach soon frightened them away again.

However, matters were brought to a head when the cockle pickers enlisted the help of a kindly witch from the village. Along the shore of Whiteford Sands, the witch drew a large circle on the beach. Within its protective circle, she then cast a secret mix of herbs and seaweed and beneath a giant full moon began to mouth a silent incantation to summon the demonic mammoth. Immediately, the mammoth could be heard charging towards the witch. Unafraid, the witch stood her ground, continuing her silent prayers. As the mammoth neared the witch, it stopped before reaching the protective circle she had inscribed in the sand around her. The behemoth stood before her, panting, obviously wary of the witch's power.

The witch, her hands held high to the full moon to draw upon its magical power, commanded the offending animal to return to the pits of hell from whence it originated. Unfortunately, at the height of the invocation, a cloud covered the full moon's face, reducing the strength of the witch's spell. And, watching the ragged animal disappear before her eyes, she sadly noted the sound of the mighty animal turn and withdraw across the bay. The spell, whilst having rid the beach of the mammoth's appearance, had not quite the power to purge the sound of the animal from the bay.

Whilst scary, the sounds created only psychological fear and, persuaded that the mammoth could no longer physically harm them, the cockle pickers returned to work.

Shellfish Collector, Whiteford Sands

Whiteford Sands

Other theories on the ghostly Whiteford Sands phenomenon speak of how the sounds originate from the spectral figures of an Iron Age tribe sprinting across the sands to repel a Roman invasion of Gower. Another tells of a local farmer, returning home in a drunken state, becoming angered by his wife's reproachful reaction and also by the fact that his missed supper now resided in the belly of his dog. His temper rose to such a degree that he physically lashed out at her. Battered and bruised, the young woman fled from the house but, enraged like never before, the drunk farmer gave chase to his wife, mounting his trusty horse to quicken the speed of his reaching her. Racing the horse as fast as he could in his inebriated and angry state, he found his wife running along Whiteford Sands. Although there was no moon to light his path, his wife's sobs ahead easily guided his way. Riled to boiling point and mocking her cries as he approached behind her fast, the farmer did not stop when he reached the woman. Instead, he drove his horse into the woman, grinding her body into the sand as, turning his horse, again and again, he pounded it to a bloodied pulp. Such was the violence on the beach that night that the act was forever imprinted on the area. And, on nights where conditions permit, the angry farmer can still be heard to this day riding his horse repeatedly over the battered body of his wife.

It is now time for us to leave Gower's northern coastline. and head to the peninsula's western fringe, starting with Llangennith...

Llangennith Hauntings

Llangennith Church

One of Gower's more far-flung villages, Llangennith has more than its share of ghostly goings-on. One apparition in particular even led to the village being published in Britain's Top Ten list of haunted roads (*Fortean Times magazine, 2001*).

Llangennith's Woman in White has been spotted even in recent times. Her original haunting ground was outside St. Cenydd's Church, meandering around its rustic gravestones. But in more recent times, the apparition has been reported on several occasions haunting the road leading from the village to Rhossili. The ethereal and luminescent figure has terrified numerous motorists with her odd habit of dashing out in front of motor vehicles. Several drivers have even slammed on their breaks to avoid a collision with the woman, only to find their cars passing through the figure as though she was not there!

Llangennith's old public house, *The King's Head*, is also reputedly haunted. A deceased landlord of the pub is still believed by many to hold residence in the property. Other patrons have also reported seeing the ghost of a startled young girl frequenting the establishment.

The King's Head, Llangennith

The King's Head, Llangennith

Returning to Llangennith Church for a moment, the ghost of the somewhat notorious John Ponsonby Lucas - Llangennith's first Reverend, is also said to haunt the village. Lucas' superior attitude and dislike of the villagers in his flock led many of their number to leave the Church. We can only imagine the horror that many of these (ex)parishioners would have felt had they known that the Reverend's presence would continue to haunt their descendants for many years after his death. Ponsonby lived in the windswept Rectory located along the sands between Llangennith and Rhossili. As such, I will keep the details of Ponsonby's rather dramatic haunting for discussion in the next section of *Gower Ghosts*.

Rhossili Bay and Rectory

Curiosities seem to abound in the village of Rhossili. First, there is the serpentine islet of Worm's Head. Could a more strange and fascinating formation of rock be imagined by even the most gifted of sculptors? And then there are the skeletal shipwrecks of the *Vernani* and the *Helvetia*, whose decaying bones still puncture the smooth sands of Rhossili Bay. How many tales of human heartache are remembered by these fading relics of centuries past? No tree of any significant size grows in the village - the place is too windswept and its air too salty for them to survive on the Atlantic-facing western fringe of the peninsula. Elderly residents, however, may remember one particular large Ash tree that once prospered in Rhossili by growing horizontally along the ground!

The Ribs of Several Wrecked Ships Protrude from the Sand on Rhossili Bay

Rhossili Downs and Worm's Head

But another curiosity perhaps piques the interest and raises the imagination above all else in Rhossili. Beneath the cliffs and its massive downs, dwarfed by the expanse of moor and sand and ocean that engulfs it, lies a windswept and lonely building - an old parsonage/rectory. Full of ghostly tales, the small building seems to swell a wild romanticism within the heart of all who see it. Its spell in the last Century captured Dylan Thomas - it nearly became the home of the poet instead of the now famous Boathouse in Laugharne. Rumour has it that only its distance from the villagepub eventually led him away from the building :-)

The Old Rectory, Rhossili

The Old Rectory, Rhossili

Mystery seems to cling to the house. Why was it built in such an isolated location? Who lived in it? Who owns it now? But even after answering these questions, having laid bare all the facts about the parsonage and its history, its intrinsic enigma remains.

The Old Rectory, Rhossili

The present-day house, designed as a rectory/parsonage, was built in 1850 upon an earlier farmstead. Its central position was seen as ideal for the Rector of the day, who had to serve the parishes of both Llangennith and Rhossili, each located at opposite ends of the bay. Its lonely setting amidst such a Romantic landscape cannot help but foster the impression that the house is haunted, and its history does not disappoint further enquiry.

The longest residing vicar of the parsonage was the Reverend John Ponsonby Lucas, who served as Rector here between 1855-1898. Given the distance between the various parishes and his home, the Reverend rode a dark stallion to carry out his duties. The vicar cut quite a figure during stormy evenings, whipping his steed along the gloomy sands amidst the howling wind and raging tide, and it is not unknown for the Reverend's spirit to be spotted even today continuing his ghostly journey between his parishes. His is not the only phantom to be seen along these sands, however.

The Old Rectory, Rhossili

Another Reverend, serving the parishes between the world wars, reported the Rectory itself was haunted. Hearing some movement on the stairs there, he was then confronted by the ghosts of an Edwardian couple. The Reverend stated that the couple moved within touching distance before disappearing into thin air. A decidedly odd aspect to these ghosts was that their skins held both an elephant hide's colour and texture!

Over the years, numerous vicars have spoken of something unpleasant coming out of the ocean at night and skulking into the parsonage and pockets of frigid air were common reoccurrences in the house. One Rector even fled from the building after feeling an unworldly presence enter the house, only then to hear a spectral voice ask, "Why don't you turn around and look at me?"

Rhossili's Old Rectory, Viewed from Llangennith Sands

After a new parsonage was built closer to Rhossili

Church, the old Rectory stood unoccupied by any mortal soul until the National Trust purchased the property in 1995 and renovated it as a holiday home.

Rhossili Bay

On particularly wild nights, another ghost, this time riding a coach pulled by four horses, haunts the vast expanse of Rhossili Bay. The spectre is believed to be the ghost of Squire Mansell, a notorious Gower tyrant of his time. One day, sometime in the 19th Century, news reached the squire that a shallow tide had revealed a treasure trove of gold along the bay. Charging to the beach, he forced his coach and horses along the sand, driving the other treasure-seekers from the bay so that he could claim the bulk of the gold for himself. Afterwards, he visited the houses of all the people he had seen on the beach and confiscated the gold they had found. With his new treasure, Mansell left Gower and was not seen again until, many years later, having squandered all of his money, he returned to Rhossili, where he was seen galloping along the bay in his coach, driven by four black steeds, searching for further treasure. His search proved fruitless. But so consumed was he with the task many believe his desperate spirit continues to explore the sands to this day.

From Rhossili we now head eastwards along Gower's southern aspect. Our first stop is near Horton, at the brow of a hill that slopes steeply down to Port Eynon Bay.

Hangman's Cross and Beggar's Pit, Cold Comfort

Hangman's Cross lies within an area known locally as Cold Comfort. Several footpaths meet here, and where the paths cross, a gibbet is believed to have once stood (O.S. 483387). Gower's last public hanging supposedly took place here, the recipient facing the noose for the crime of sheep-stealing.

South of Hangman's Cross, adjacent to the footpath, is a geological sinkhole known evocatively as Beggar's Pit (O.S. 481866). Legend says the corpses of the villains hanged at Hangman's Cross were disposed of here, although there is no archaeological evidence to support this once generally held belief. The sinkhole derives its name from the time of the Black Death, when villagers who were unable to afford a private funeral were buried here in their masses. Such a

Hangman's Cross, Cold Comfort, from Grave Lane

location seems ripe for tales of ghosts, but these seem to have been all lost to time.

Despite this, I have included the area in this guide to *Gower Ghosts* as supernatural events were once associated with the place. In C.D. Morgan's fascinating, if very anachronistic book, *Wanderings in Gower* (published in 1886), he tantalises his readers when describing having to pick up his pace to a run when passing through Cold Comfort in the hope of not bumping into the resident ghost there. Unfortunately, his particularly flowery prose refrains from including any further details of the haunting, leaving the present-day visitor to these locations uncertain about the source of any disquiet felt here. Still, the area is well worth a visit to soak up its atmosphere here and to wonder who or what is haunting Cold Comfort!

Looking Down into the Overgrown Beggar's Pit

The Ghostly Ceffyl Dŵr of Oxwich Churchyard

A Gower Pony Impersonating the Ceffyl Dŵr

The Beautifully Eerie Oxwich Church

The medieval Church of St. Illtyd must possess one of the most beautifully situated graveyards in the country. Almost buried by the giant canopy of a dense and steeply inclined wood, the Church appears to stand aloof from the village and the sandy bay it overlooks, despite being separated from them both by only a few moments' walk.

At the height of the summer season, when the sun is roasting all who bathe beneath its unblinkered stare, it is a most disquieting experience to stumble from the bustling sands into the chill and shaded solitude of the church grounds. The clammy, twilight atmosphere that clings to this churchyard transports its visitors to a ghostly other-world, a feeling that is undisturbed, perhaps even amplified, by the contrasting sound of the sun-worshipping tourists that holiday but a stone's throw from its ivy-clad walls.

Oxwich Medieval Church

Given such a picturesque and genuinely eerie setting, it is not surprising that one of the strangest ghosts on the peninsula has chosen to manifest itself here. The creature appears in the form of the Ceffyl Dŵr, the ghostly white horse from Welsh legend. The apparition, spotted on numerous occasions, haunts the graveyard itself and the beach immediately adjacent to the church. The Ceffyl Dŵr appears as a solid, if somewhat luminous, white horse who can transform into mist and disappear.

The Ceffyl Dŵr is said to enter our world from the old water spring (now dried up), located behind Oxwich Church. Whenever spotted in the churchyard, either leaving or entering the well, he is said to take to his hind legs and take the appearance of a half-man, half-horse creature.

Giant's Grave, Parkmill

We now head east along the peninsula's southern coast to Parkmill. There are a couple of sites of supernatural interest in this village. Firstly, we will take a walk out to the Neolithic long barrow tomb, known variously as Parch Le Breos Burial Chamber, Parc Cwm Long Cairn or just Giant's Grave.

We will be heading inside the Gower Heritage Centre before leaving the village, so this is an excellent place to park your car before heading into the Parc le Breos (Green Cwm) estate on foot.

Giant's Grave dates as far back as 3,500 BC and is a

classic example of a transept gallery grave. The monument consists of a long mound of stones (of local origin) with a deep forecourt at its southern extremity. A slab lined passage dissects the monument, interrupted by two pairs of side chambers. Initially roofed over with other slabs, these now lie open for public view.

Giant's Grave, Parkmill

Discovered in 1869, when workers digging for road stones came across the rocks of its central chamber, the tomb was excavated in the same year by Sir John Lubbock (famed for introducing the word Neolithic, meaning New Stone Age, into the English language). During this excavation, animal bones, Neolithic pottery and around 24 human skeletons were unearthed. These are now on display at the Ashmolean Museum (University of Oxford).

Giant's Grave, Parkmill

Burial galleries, such as Giant's Grave, were typically utilised by several generations of the Neolithic community. The deceased occupants here would have been exposed to the elements to speed their decomposition before their ceremonial burial within the tomb. The skeleton occupants of the grave were ritually dismembered and moved around as more community members needed to be accommodated there.

This site has a reputation for being haunted. It has been long noted that sheep grazing here always vacate the grounds at dusk to take shelter amongst the trees. And it is easy for the more sensitive late evening visitor to Giant's Grave to experience an ancient disquiet stir the atmosphere here. Several people have also reported seeing the ghost of a melancholy woman wandering around the tomb.

The Gower Heritage Centre

The Gower Heritage Centre, Parkmill

Next, we head to one of the Gower's major tourist attractions - the Gower Heritage Centre. There is a fee to pay before accessing the site, but there is plenty to explore inside, so an investigation of the Centre is well worth the price of an entry ticket.

The Waterwheel at GHC

The Gower Heritage Centre is designed around an 800 year old watermill Built during Norman Rule, the mill served the Parc le Breos Estate and its surrounding farms. The le Breos Estate held quite a tyrannical rule over the area and forced local farmers to use their more expensive mill rather than others, fining those who failed to do so. They also forced the farmers to pay the mill's running costs and carry out any necessary repairs to it.

The Davies family took over the mill's running in the 17th Century and continued to run the mill for a further five generations. They had to develop other skills such as smithying, woodturning, constructing cartwheels, farm gates, sawmilling, and even undertaking to keep the mill profitable.

There are multiple hauntings associated with the Gower Heritage Centre, Parkmill. Perhaps the most well-known ghost being "Will the Mill.". Will, the last of the millers at Parkmill, was one of Gower's truly great characters. As well as being a miller, wheelwright and carpenter, he also held office as local mayor. His name is now synonymous with the mill, so much so that an effigy of

Grave concerns at the Gower Heritage Centre, Parkmill

"Will the Mill" – a Ghostly Resident of The Gower Heritage Centre, Parkmill

him can still be seen at the Gower Heritage Centre today, sat at his table as a recorded interview with him, held by Wynford Vaughan Thomas, plays from the radio at his side. There have been numerous sightings of his ghost near the old watermill. Unfortunately, these always take place at either 7 a.m. or 7 p.m., outside the regular opening hours of the Centre.

Parkmill's Haunted Leat

"Will the Mill" is not the only ghost said to haunt the Gower Heritage Centre. The spirit of a young woman also lingers here. Seen racing along the Mill Leat, the channel that leads water from the adjacent stream at a high level to drop down and operate the large waterwheel, the ghost appears panicked, chased by a man wielding a heavy medieval sword.

Whilst the woman's identity is not known, she is believed to have belonged to the entourage of Lady Malephant—wife of Sir Thomas Malephant of Pembroke.

Lady Malephant was visiting her sister at Parkmill when she and her group met an ambush. Engineered by Lewes Leyshon - who wanted Lady Malephant as his wife, he directed and paid Sir Gilbert de Turbeville to wait behind the Mill with his thugs. Unbeknown to Lady Malephant, news had reached Leyshon that Lady Malephant's husband had just died, and he saw this ambush as an ideal way to force her hand into marriage.

The struggle between Sir Gilbert de Turberville's men and Lady Malephant's servants was bloody. One of Lady Malephant's maidservants, Agnes, had her arm amputated by a swordsman during the struggle, and at least one member of the entourage was killed. The injured, left behind after lady Malephant's abduction, took refuge within the mill, where they were duly charged for their care by the miller. Lady Malephant was imprisoned in a castle and held in degrading circumstances until she finally agreed to marry Lewes Leyshon. At this stage, she managed to send word to the king of what had taken place. An investigation found Leyshon guilty of murder and other crimes related to the ambush and also the illegal imprisonment of Lady Malephant. Lewes Leyshon was duly executed.

As if two ghosts associated with one property were not enough, a third apparition also haunts the Gower Heritage Centre. This ghost is believed to be one of the Davies' Family children who was crushed to death after falling from the will window onto the waterwheel sometime in the 19th Century. The window has now been bricked up, but the child's ghost continues to be seen above the Millwheel as if the window was still in existence.

With the waterwheel unable to complete with modern

flour production techniques, sawmill activity kept the mill open longer than any other of Gower's grist mills. However, when this too closed in 1983, it seemed that an end to an era had arrived. However, within six years, the Gower Heritage Centre took over the property, bringing the waterwheel and its adjacent smithy back to life. Thanks to this tourist attraction, not to mention the mill's three resident ghosts, it appears this unique slice of Gower's history will forever be remembered.

Pennard Castle

Pennard Castle from Pennard Pill

Perched high over the magnificent Three Cliffs Bay, the mysterious Pennard Castle has to be one of the most picturesque ruins on the Gower Peninsula. The recorded history of the 13th-century stronghold is scant, but it is known that its occupancy was short-lived. With few historical documents to detail the site, the castle bathes in an air of superstition, with many legends and folktales noting the castle to be both haunted and cursed!

Pennard Castle from Three Cliffs Bay

Given its location and mysterious history, it was only natural for tales of ghosts and other supernatural occurrences to attach themselves to the castle. Perhaps the most famous of these hauntings is the Gwrach-y-rhibyn – a banshee who roams the castle grounds, condemning all those who dare spend a night amongst the enigmatic ruins to instant madness!

Pennard Castle, Overlooking Three Cliffs and Oxwich Bays

Viewed on a hot summer's day, with its breath-taking scenery delighting the senses, such tales can seem incredulous. But alone on darker, stormy winter evenings, with the chill wind howling about the cragged castle walls, this place can genuinely stir the imagination. Even if still not fully believed, it is possible in those moments of brooding solitude to truly appreciate the hidden world of magic that has for so long dominated the countryside, not only here at Pennard but in the Gower peninsula as a whole.

Pwlldu

Pwlldu Bay

Said to haunt Pwlldu's old *Beaufort Inn* and the surrounding valley is the ghost of a young teenage mother. The apparition is that of a young woman, unable to cope with

Pwlldu Bridge, Scene of a Suicide that Led to the Area's Haunting

Pwlldu Bridge – The Most Common Manifestation Spot of the 'Lady in White'

early motherhood, who drowned herself in the Bishopston stream. The ghost is dressed in a long white dress and clutches her tiny baby to her breast. Spotted fairly regularly since 1860, she has also been reported by tourists unfamiliar with this haunting.

Forwarded by an occupant of one of the bay's isolated cottages, a more recent theory about this apparition identifies the ghost as that of an old lady named Rachel Timothy. Rachel lived in the neighbouring cottage and died when her house caught fire.

Overnight visitors of the present-day incumbents at Pwlldu have reported feeling very uneasy during the night whilst staying there.

The Isolated Cottages of Pwlldu Bay

Other ghosts have also been reported at Pwlldu, with numerous recorded sightings of "dark figures" walking across the beach at night. These are believed to be the ghosts of infamous smugglers who once operated on this bay.

The Screaming Lady of Brandy Cove

Brandy Cove

Perhaps less well known than the tales of smuggling more usually associated with Brandy Cove are the incidences of the supernatural connected with the beach

The ghost connected with Brandy Cove has a chilling

link with a real-life murder, which took place on or near the beach during the winter of 1919. First reported by a couple walking along the cliffs above Brandy Cove one evening, - stories of a woman's screams, echoing through the cliffs numerous caves and abandoned mines, became everyday talk amongst the surrounding villages of Pennard, Bishopston and Caswell. These tales soon burgeoned, with the locals becoming too afraid to visit the beach after dark.

Matters came to a head in 1961 when several Bishopston youths decided to give the caves of Brandy Cove a thorough exploration. It did not take them too long to uncover a horrifying secret.

There, hidden behind a wall of boulders in an old lead mine, they discovered the skeletal remains of Mamie Stuart - a young woman who had disappeared from the area more than forty years earlier. Although her killer never faced justice, the evidence strongly suggests that the young chorus girl died at the hands of her jealous bigamist husband, George Shotton. With so many years having passed between her death and the discovery of her remains, no soft tissue remained on the skeleton, and no actual cause of death could be ascertained. However, what was easily discernible was that Mamie's body had been inexpertly cut into three large pieces before being walled into the mine.

The resulting police investigation immediately brought up George Shotton as the chief, if not only, suspect in the case. Unfortunately, Shotton was never brought to trial as he died of natural causes in 1958, aged 78 years - just three years before the discovery of Mamie's remains. Although justice never seems to have been meted over her murder, it is believed that Mamie's soul is now at peace as, after her discovery, no ghostly cries were heard here again.

Caswell's Ghostly Sand Castle

Caswell Bay

Now lost to the ravages of time, Bishopston's old Rectory was the scene of a curious exorcism of a 'white lady.' The sole human occupant of the Rectory was the village's elderly widowed Rector, and he was plagued by the apparition of an old woman dressed in white for several months. Whence she had come, he had no idea for her unwelcome company was as sudden as it was fearful. The first time he witnessed the ghost, it had taken the form of a light, spectral mist, but the presence became more solid and utterly terrifying with each successive visitation. On later occasions, he was able to detail her features very precisely -

her sallow complexion and burning eyes being of particular note amongst his descriptions of the ghost. Later still, the visits were accompanied by the low murmur of a heartbeat. By the height of her reign of terror, this murmur had increased in volume so that the whole house seemed to echo with the pounding of her heart. It was not long before furniture in the Rectory also started to rattle and sway with her accompanying visitations.

The Rector brought many people to the Rectory to witness the ghost for themselves. But whenever he had company, the White Lady failed to appear. It was not long before a reputation of senility started to cloud people's view of the Rector. So it was with great relief when, one day, a gipsy woman, having called upon the Rectory to sell her wares, stepped back aghast, crying "Ghost. Ghost" as he opened the door to her call.

The Rector, aware of the knowledge of spells and such things held by gipsies, took the old woman by her hands and begged her to help him rid the spirit from his home. Agreeing, she told the Rector of a ceremony that might be useful to his needs.

The Rector immediately set to work on the exorcism and, following the gipsy woman's ceremony to the letter, brought 12 men of the Church to his home. Gathered around a table, upon which stood 12 bells and 12 lit candles, the men waited for the clock to strike the hour of midnight. Ghosts, the gipsy woman had told the Rector, had an affinity for darkness, and the White Lady would attempt to put out the candles during the ceremony. Should the ghost succeed in extinguishing the flame from every candle on the table before the last stroke of midnight sounded then, the exorcism would fail. However, if the men could manage to confuse the spirit with the ringing of the bells and their various incantations to God, the ghost would be forced to vacate the Rectory forever.

Midnight approached with a growing sense of unease and silence. The congregation's mood grew sombre and intense with the first chord of the 'witching hour'. This time, even though the Rector now had company, the men's prayers summoned the ghost to the room. The room's silence broke with the sound of a thundering heartbeat, and the furniture around the group began to shake. But, despite their fear, each man held steadfast to the purpose of their task. Heading straight for the table, the White Lady rushed to snuff out the candles. Extinguishing the first one quickly in her rage, the men now sounded their handbells. Immediately the White Lady became disorientated and confused, just as the old gipsy woman had promised. With the last strike of the clock, candles still flickered in the room, and the ghost stood quiet as she awaited the punishment of the Rector. With her fate announced, the White Lady fled the Rectory to begin the labour to which she had been condemned.

In the central portion of Caswell Bay, near the point where the river meets the sea, today's visitors may witness a strange stirring in the sand and hear a curious whisper carried on the wind. For this is the spot where the White Lady now undertakes the laborious and never-ending task, set to her by the Rector and his men, of building a sandcastle capable of withstanding the tide's ebb and flow.

Caswell Bay

The Bubbling Puddle, Caswell Bay

Bob's Cave, Mumbles

Bob's Cave, Mumbles

On Mumbles' outer headland, hidden from mainland gaze, a gaping sea cavern lies beneath the foundations of Mumbles Lighthouse. Known as Bob's Cave, the cavern is named after Bob Jenkins, the Mumbles Lifeboat crew member who was washed into the cave during an ill-fated sea rescue attempt in January 1883. So obscured is the cave from the land, and so awkward is it to reach, that Bob had to survive for two whole days in the cavern before finally being discovered.

The remains of bison and buffalo found in the cave, dating from Neolithic times, provide evidence that it once had far easier access than it has today.

Despite the relative inaccessibility of Bob's Cave, an elderly monk once used it as a monastic cell. Although living a hermit-like existence, this monk occasionally came into contact with other people. It was the result of one of these meetings that gave rise to the ghostly tale now attached to the cave. The old monk had been sat at the entrance to the cave, watching the beautiful colours the sea had grasped from the setting sun. Amongst the rippling bands of gold and red and yellow, the monk spied a rowing boat and soon realised that it was making its way towards him. As the boat neared, the two oarsmen called to him and asked the old monk's aid in relieving them of the dead body that lay on the floor of the boat. As the monk helped pull the body of the well-dressed man into the shelter of the cave, he grew suspicious that the two oarsmen had murdered the gentleman for his money. This suspicion grew when the oarsmen handed the monk some coins to pay him for some prayers to enable the dead man's soul to find peace—a request designed to ease the oarsmen's conscience, the monk believed. He also suspected that the few coins offered him originated from the dead man's own pockets. Unwilling to let the dead man's soul suffer, the old monk accepted the body and began his prayers as the two vagabonds rowed away to sea again. But whatever prayers the old monk offered that evening, they must not have sufficed to compensate for the dreadful death the well-dressed man had suffered. For, to this day, it is said that his wails of unrest can still be heard issuing forth from the cavern.

The cave gained a little notoriety in the 18th Century when the pirate Joseph Avery was hanged at the entrance in 1731.

Oystermouth Castle

Oystermouth Castle is the Gower Peninsula's most haunted castle, and there have been countless reports of a ghostly woman in white appearing outside the fortification's ancient walls. A gentleman, letting his dog off its lead to have a run around the castle's spacious grounds, was surprised to see his pet suddenly race towards him from behind a tree in obvious terror. Curious about what had caused the animal's fright, the man walked over to the tree where he saw what he first figured to be a large white sheet resting on the grass near the tree's trunk. As he approached the sheet, however, it suddenly started from the ground and took the form of a woman wearing a white robe. She then faded from sight like dissolving mist.

Oystermouth Castle

Not a happy figure, this apparition is nearly always seen sobbing, with her head drooped into her palms as she weeps. Some people who have encountered Oystermouth Castle's "Woman in White" have also been unlucky enough to view the cause of this poor woman's suffering.

Oystermouth Castle

A family picnicking on the grounds were dismayed when their young children appeared from behind a tree screaming. When asked what had frightened them so, they explained that they had seen a lady dressed in a long white robe with a cord fastened around her waist. She appeared to the children as if she had been sobbing, although she had made no actual sound whatsoever. Perturbed by their story, the children's father then went to the tree to see the woman in white for himself. She was still there as he approached the tree, but seeing his approach, the figure turned its back to the man. It was then that the father witnessed that the back of the woman's dress had been ripped apart and that her naked back had been shredded and bled with lacerations.

Oystermouth Castle's Stone Whipping Post

It is thought that the ghost of the "woman in white" dates from Medieval times and had been a prisoner of Oystermouth Castle who had been flogged to death on the whipping post, which still stands in the castle's large dungeon.

Conclusion

With the turning of the seasons, as the early dusky evenings retreat and the skeletal trees bud and flower with the growing heat of spring, then summer, it will be easy, once more, to forget the imaginative tales of Gower's Great, Great Grandparents. Amongst the colour and in/activity of a typical Gower beach every sunny weekend in August, it may even appear absurd that such stories were once popular amongst the peninsula's residents.

The character and very nature of Gower continues to change. It is not a defeatist's attitude to admit to the fact. Everything moves on. The old always gives way to the new. Despite the exemplary work of local conservation and heritage organisations to slow the process, Gower can never be saved from the relentless march of time.

Whereas the aural folktale once entertained families, now it is the turn of multi-national satellite broadcasters to fire and stir the population's imaginations. It is arguable to state, one way or another, whether it provides a good service at this. But one fact that can be noted is that the local diversity of entertainment and story-telling has been lost to the 21st Century world. Whilst this will, in all probability, never return, it is undoubtedly essential to keep alive those traditions of yesteryear lest they be buried forever along with our forefathers who spent so much time creating and embroidering them. I hope this short guide helps in addressing this concern.

Chris Elphick

ABOUT THE AUTHOR

Chris Elphick grew up in the village of Penclawdd, located on the northern coast of the Gower Peninsula. He studied Art and Design at Gower College, Swansea and gained a BA (Hons) degree in photography at the West Surrey College of Art and Design.

Chris is the author of numerous folk-horror novels, photography zines and The Verry Volk ~ Faery Folklore of the Gower Peninsula.

For further information on his various writing and photography projects, please visit:

pixie-led.co.uk

Also by Chris Elphick

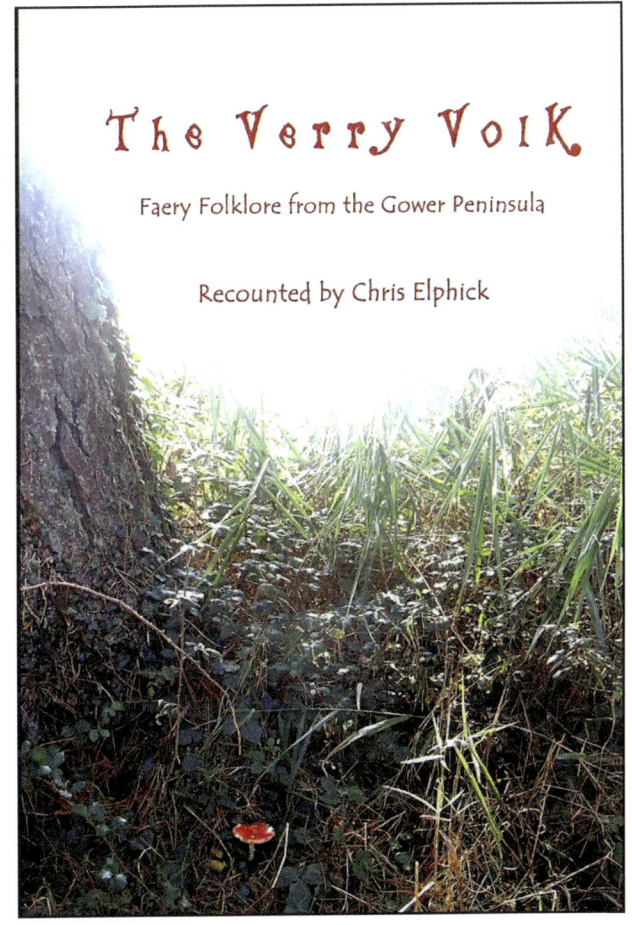

Printed in Great Britain
by Amazon